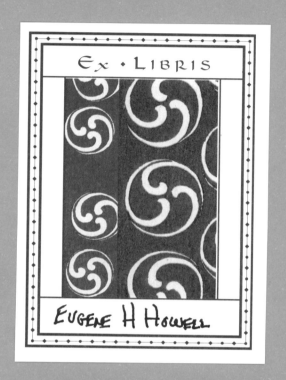

Ex · Libris

Eugene H Howell

LIGHTHOUSES

AROUND
THE WORLD

COURAGE BOOKS

AN IMPRINT OF RUNNING PRESS
PHILADELPHIA • LONDON

9 8 7 6 5 4 3 2 1

Digit on the right indicates the number of this printing.

ISBN 0-7624-0992-4

Cataloging-in-Publication Number 00-135108

Designed by Corinda Cook
Edited by Melissa Wagner
Introduction by Heather Henson
Text researched by Catherine Sweeney
Photos researched by Jane Sanders
The text was set in Berthold Bodoni, Bodoni Old Face,
and Poppl-Residenz

Published by Courage Books, an imprint of
Running Press Book Publishers
125 South Twenty-second Street
Philadelphia, Pennsylvania 19103-4399

This book may be ordered by mail from the publisher.
Please include $2.50 for postage and handling.
But try your bookstore first!

Visit us on the web!
www.runningpress.com

INTRODUCTION

*S*ince the beginning of time, men and women have been drawn to the sea—for adventure, for profit, for a chance to begin life anew on some distant shore. And for as long as there have been voyagers on the rivers and lakes and oceans of the world, there have been beacons to help guide them to safety.

Thousands of years ago, Greeks, Romans, Egyptians, and Phoenicians lit bonfires on hilltops and cliffs to help guide their sailors along treacherous shores. The earliest references to such beacons are found in the *Iliad* and the *Odyssey*, both written in the eighth century B.C.

As time passed, people began to realize that elevated fires could be seen from a greater distance and so they began to build wood or stone towers with tended fires burning at the top. Around 280 B.C., the Egyptians built the first great lighthouse in history, the Pharos of Alexandria.

The Pharos stood 450 feet tall—at the time the tallest structure in the world. For centuries it guided ships to the world's busiest seaport, and even today, it lives on in the language of the sea. In France, the word for lighthouse is *phare;* in Spain and Italy, *faro.* In English, the study of lighthouse technology is "pharology."

The Romans were next. As they began to expand their vast empire, they built a system of lighthouses along the coasts of Asia, Africa, and Europe. Ruins of their well-built structures can still be seen today on the shores of France and Great Britain. The Phoenicians, a great seafaring people, sailed to distant lands as well, establishing a trading route marked by beacons to safeguard their ships filled with precious cargo.

Lighthouse construction slowed during the Dark Ages, when there was a sharp decline in travel and trade. But by 1100, Italy and France were taking the lead in lighthouse design and construction, and Great Britain was following suit, establishing beacons along its coasts and dotting its colonies with light. By 1716, Boston Light—America's first lighthouse—was built by the Massachusetts Bay colonists at the entrance to Boston Harbor.

The nineteenth and twentieth centuries saw huge advances in lighthouse design and engineering. But slowly, modern technology began to eclipse the need for visual navigational aides. Today's ships navigate using radar and satellites and other invisible, powerful signals. More and more, lighthouses are being transformed into museums and parks—shining beacons to the world's past.

Throughout history, lighthouses have held a special place in our hearts and minds. They are mysterious yet comforting structures. They are symbols of adventure and despair, monuments to humanity's innate wanderlust and to our helplessness in the face of nature.

Old Point Loma Lighthouse (left and above) guided ships at the entrance of the San Diego Harbor from November of 1855 until March of 1891. At 422 feet above sea level, Point Loma seemed the perfect place for a lighthouse. In 1851, the United States Coastal Survey chose the sight because a lighthouse there could guide ships on the Pacific Ocean as well as those sailing into the harbor. However, once the lighthouse was operational, sailors discovered a serious problem with the seemingly ideal location—because it was so high above the sea, ships often couldn't see the light through fog and clouds. Since the station was not equipped with a foghorn, it is said that Captain Robert Decatur Israel, keeper of Point Loma for eighteen years, would fire a shotgun to warn passing ships of the dangerous rocks in the harbor. Eventually, the fight against the fog proved futile, so the lighthouse was decommissioned. A new lighthouse was built at a lower elevation, closer to the water at the bottom of the hill (this lighthouse is pictured on pages 54–55). The Old Point Loma Lighthouse still stands watch over the San Diego Harbor, now as a part of the Cabrillo National Monument. The National Park Service restored the interior of the lighthouse to its original 1800s decor, and the lighthouse serves as a museum dedicated to educating visitors about a bygone era and its interesting history.

Au Sable Lighthouse (top and right), one of the most remote mainland lightstations in North America, is located about twelve miles from Grand Marais, Michigan, in Pictured Rocks National Lakeshore along Lake Superior. The lighthouse was built in 1874 to light the dark and treacherous eighty-mile stretch of water between Grand Island Lighthouse and the Whitefish Point Lighthouse. There is no direct road to the Au Sable Light, so visitors have to hike a 1.5 mile trail along which the wreckage of several ships may be seen. The remains of these ships serve as a reminder of the power held by Lake Superior, one of the most dangerous lakes in the United States.

(bottom) Lighthouse overlooking the St. Lawrence Seaway near Place Royale, Quebec City, Canada.

(overleaf) **South Mole Lighthouse** (foreground) and **North Mole Lighthouse** (background) keep watch over Fremantle Harbor, sometimes called "the gateway to Australia." The twin towers have guided ships through the harbor since the turn of the century—South Mole with a fixed green light, and North Mole with a fixed red light. The colors were chosen to avoid confusion with the brilliant white beacon cast by nearby Woodman Point Leading Light.

The Rostral Columns, located on the Strelka (Spit) of Vasilevsky Island in St. Petersburg, Russia, can be seen from the tzar's former residence, the Winter Palace. The two Rostral Columns flank the former Stock Exchange, which was designed by French architect Thomas de Thomon and built between 1805–1810. The columns are adorned with ships' prows, and though they served as navigational beacons in the nineteenth century, today their gas torches are lit only on some public holidays.

The sea hath no king but God alone.

From "The White Ship"
Dante Gabriel Rossetti (1828–1882)
English poet and painter

(top) **Firkas Tower** stands watch over the Venetian Harbor in Venice, Italy.

(bottom) **El Faro (The Lighthouse)** is a popular restaurant and tourist destination in Marina Vallarta, just north of Puerto Vallarta, Mexico. The tower stretches 110 feet in the air, and features a glass elevator on the outside of the structure which leads to a circular lounge—the perfect spot to relax and enjoy a beautiful sunset overlooking Marina Vallarta and the Bay of Banderas.

(top) The lighthouse on the small island of Eilean Ban was built in the mid-nineteenth century by the father of *Treasure Island* novelist Robert Louis Stevenson. Also known as "White Island," Eilean Ban lies between the Isle of Skye and mainland Scotland, under the Isle of Skye Bridge. The island is now a community-run wildlife sanctuary.

(bottom) **Garcia Dávila** has lit the waters near Praia do Forte, Bahia, Brazil, since 1816.

(right) **Gibb's Hill Lighthouse** in Southampton Parish, Bermuda, is one of the oldest cast-iron lighthouses in the world. Construction on the lighthouse began in 1844 in response to more than thirty-nine shipwrecks in the area within an unreasonably short period of time. According to legend, when the lighthouse was lit for the first time, Southampton's residents threw out their whale-oil lanterns and candles in the belief that it would forever light their nights. In fact, some locals still refer to the lighthouse as the "Parish Lantern," following the tradition started by their predecessors from the nineteenth century. Gibb's Hill Lighthouse stands 117 feet tall, shining its beacon 362 feet above sea level. It is still in operation, and guides ships as far as forty miles out to sea, as well as airplane pilots flying at ten thousand feet above sea level as far as 120 miles away.

(overleaf) **Le Phare de Tevennec**, in Cap Sizun in the French Polynesian archipelagos.

(left) **The Lighthouse of Barra**, in the city of Salvador, Brazil, sits atop the Fort of Saint Anthony of Barra, the oldest fort in the city. Construction on the fort began in 1580 on the tip of the peninsula in northeastern Brazil. The lighthouse was restored in 1998, and now houses a marine museum.

(right) **Santa Marta Lighthouse**, in Laguna, Santa Catarina, Brazil, features a very big lens atop the stairs shown in this picture—it weighs about one ton, and has a diameter of about fifteen feet.

Oh dream of joy, is this indeed
The lighthouse top I see?
Is this the hill? is this the kirk?
Is this mine own countree?

**From *The Rime of the Ancient Mariner*
Samuel Coleridge (1772–1834)
English poet**

(left) **Celerain Lighthouse** sits at the southernmost tip of the island of Cozumel, Mexico.

(top, left) **Ocracoke Light** stands on historic Ocracoke Island in North Carolina, where British forces captured and killed the notorious pirate Blackbeard in the early eighteenth century. The lighthouse pictured here was built in 1823, and is the second oldest operating lighthouse in the United States. It stands seventy-five feet tall, and casts a stationary white beam that can be seen fourteen miles at sea, guiding ships through the often tricky waters of the shoal-ridden inlet of the Outer Banks. The diameter of the lighthouse narrows from twenty-five feet at the base to twelve feet at the top—the walls are made of brick, twelve feet thick at the bottom tapering to two feet at the peak. Because of this, the lighthouse has successfully weathered several hurricanes. The Fresnel lens was dismantled by Confederate soldiers early in the Civil War, but it was reconstructed in 1864 by Union forces.

(top, right) **Detail of Fresnel lens** at Islas San Benito, Mexico. In 1828, Frenchman Augustin Jean Fresnel invented the most efficient lens ever used in lighthouses. Experimenting with a drop of honey over a small hole cut out of cardboard, Fresnel discovered a way to magnify light rays into a single powerful beam. Before Fresnel's invention, the best lamp—which was actually several lamps put together—could produce a light of about twenty thousand candlepower. With Fresnel's lens, it increased to eighty thousand candlepower. Eventually the introduction of electric power allowed Fresnel's lens to intensify one light to more than one million candlepower.

(overleaf) **Pemaquid Point Light**, in Bristol, Maine, marks a dramatic entrance to the Muscongus Bay and John Bay, with its streaks of granite reaching for the sea. Pemaquid Point was the scene for many a shipwreck before a lighthouse was finally commissioned in 1826, including the remarkable ruin of the English ship *Angel Gabriel* in 1635, in which five passengers to the New World were killed on the rocks, and the surviving one hundred passengers lost all of their belongings. One especially gripping story is that of a man who sailed on the *Angel Gabriel* and barely escaped the sinking ship with his life. His wife was to follow him from England after he established a new life in the colonies, but because of the accident she was too afraid to make the perilous journey. He couldn't bring himself to sail again either, so they died without seeing each other again. The first lighthouse at Pemaquid Point didn't last for more than a few years, possibly because the builder may have used salt water to mix his mortar. A new tower was built in 1835, and the light was fully automated in 1934. It is still in use today, guiding ships into the rough, cold waters of the bays.

(top) **Guia Lighthouse** in the stylish city of Cascais, Portugal. In the sixteenth century, Cascais was a small fishing village, but was said to be the guardian of Lisbon because it was the first land to be seen by navigators as they arrived in and departed from Portugal from trips on the high seas. It was at this time that one of the world's first lighthouses was built, at the very same spot where the Guia Lighthouse shines its beacon today.

(right) **Big Tub Light** has marked the entrance to Big Tub Harbor in Tobermory, Ontario, Canada, since 1885. In the 1870s, before the lighthouse was built, an early settler to the area, Charles Earl, hung a lantern on a tree at the same spot where the lighthouse was later built in an attempt to show ships the way into the harbor. Earl became the first keeper of the lighthouse in 1885. Despite his efforts and those of the keepers which followed him in the line of duty, there have been more than twenty-one shipwrecks in the area, all of which can be seen by glass-bottom boat tours in Fathom Five National Park, Ontario, Canada.

(left) **Faro Formentor** in Cape Formentor, home to one of the world's largest living coral reefs, off the beautiful Spanish island of Ibiza.

(this page) There are two lighthouses at **Cape Point** on the Cape of Good Hope, South Africa. The oldest lighthouse, which is pictured to the left, was built in the 1850s on Cape Point Peak, 780 feet above sea level. However, because it was built so high, the lighthouse was often obscured by clouds and fog. The sinking of the Portuguese ocean liner *Lusitania* on April 18, 1911, forced the decision to build another Cape Point Lighthouse at its present location closer to the water, only 285 feet above sea level. At 10 million candlepower, the new lighthouse (shown above) boasts the most powerful beam on the coast of South Africa.

(left) Lighthouse on Ærø Island, a sleepy 6- by 22-mile island off the southern edge of Denmark.

(top) **Preguiças Farol**, in Barreirinhas, in the state of Maranhão, Brazil.

(bottom) **Portland Head Light** in Cape Elizabeth, Maine, has watched over the Casco Bay since George Washington appointed its first keeper in 1791. Though it has been eighty feet tall since 1882, the tower underwent many changes in height during its first hundred years of operation, and the building retains the scars formed by its many changes in stature. Today, Portland Head Light, where Longfellow penned his famous poem "The Lighthouse," is one of Maine's most popular tourist destinations.

(overleaf) **Farol Ponta da St. Vicente**, at Cape St. Vicente, a southern peninsula in Portugal.

(left, above, and overleaf) **Heceta Head Lighthouse**, located in Devil's Elbow State Park along the Pacific Coast Highway in Oregon, is considered by many to be one of the most beautiful lighthouses in the world. The lighthouse remains in use—its beacon can be seen as far as twenty-one miles out to sea, making it the brightest light on the Oregon coast. Both the lighthouse and the beautiful Victorian-style keeper's house were built in 1894 for an impressive $180,000, which was quite a large sum at the time. The keeper's house is now a bed and breakfast, and many say the house is haunted. Legend has it that a young child died in the house in the 1890s, and that the ghost of either the child or the child's mother (nobody is certain which) has haunted the residence ever since. Nearly all of the residents of the house have reported unexplainable things, including screams and things found moved or missing. Perhaps the most interesting story belongs to a worker who was cleaning windows in the attic. He noticed a reflection in the glass and turned around to see a silver-haired woman in a long, black dress. He ran out and refused to work in the attic ever again. He later accidentally broke the glass in an attic window when cleaning outside, but would not go in to clean up the glass. That night, the couple living at the station heard noises in the attic, and when they went upstairs the next day they found that the glass had been swept unexplainably into a pile.

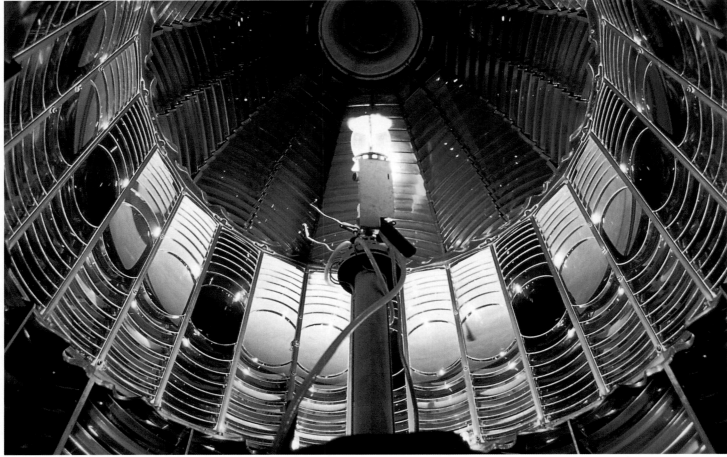

(top) **Detail of mechanism** at Farol Arvoredo, Florianopolis, Santa Caterina, Brazil.

(bottom) **Detail of the lamp** at Farol da Barra, Salvador, Bahia, Brazil.

(right) **Cabot Head Lighthouse**, near the northern tip of the Bruce Peninsula in Ontario, Canada, looks out on white limestone cliffs and the clear water of the Georgian Bay.

(left and top) **Salinopolis Belem**, in the state of Pará, Brazil, is a 128-feet-tall structure built in 1852 which includes more than twelve thousand screws. Its light beams more than forty-five miles out to sea.

(bottom) **Louisbourg Lighthouse** near Sydney, Cape Breton Island, in Nova Scotia, Canada. The lighthouse shown here is actually the third lighthouse built in this location. The first was built by the French in 1731, after one of the king of France's ships, *Le Profond*, nearly met its demise entering the harbor. The lighthouse was the first built in Canada, and the second in North America (the first was built in Boston Harbor in 1716). It caught fire in 1736, was rebuilt, and functioned for twenty years, until the second British seige in 1758. At that point the light was deemed beyond repair and left to disintegrate. A second lighthouse was constructed by the British in 1842, but it met the same fiery ruin as the first lighthouse. The tower which watches the harbor today has stood guard since 1923, but the ruins of the eighteenth- and nineteenth-century lighthouses still exist nearby as reminders of the history of the harbor.

(top) **Mystic Seaport Light**, in Mystic, Connecticut, is a replica of Nantucket's Brant Point Light, which is shown on page one of this book. Mystic Seaport sits right on the Mystic River, which made it a perfect whaling and shipbuilding center during the nineteenth century. The town is now a major tourist center, and features a notable collection of historic ships in addition to the many traveling tall ships it welcomes to its harbor every year.

(left) **Cape Hatteras Light**, located on the Outer Banks of the North Carolina seashore, is the tallest in the United States, an immense 193 feet from the edge of the sidewalk at the entrance to the top of the roof. The familiar beacon guides sailors through the "Graveyard of the Atlantic," the treacherous reefs of the Diamond Shoals. Before lighthouses were built along the Outer Banks, the absence of natural landmarks on the Carolina Coast forced sailors dangerously close to shore before they could determine where they were, and as many as five hundred ships have been stuck near Cape Hatteras throughout the years. That is why the structure has such a recognizable appearance—by day, its black-and-white stripes are visible for miles. At night, the revolving beacon can be seen about twenty miles out to sea. From the beginning, coastal erosion has threatened Cape Hatteras Light. In 1870, the lighthouse was placed more than two hundred feet from the water, but constant erosion threatened the stability of the Light. In the late summer of 1999, the Cape Hatteras Light was moved farther inland from the ocean's battering waves.

(right) **West Quoddy Head Light** in Lubec, Maine, marks the easternmost point in the United States—it is the first spot in the U.S. at which the sun can be seen each morning.

(left) Fishing at **Robertson Point Lighthouse**, New South Wales, Australia.

(top) **St. David's Lighthouse** overlooks the south shore of St. David's Island, in St. George, Bermuda. At fifty-five feet tall, it is the smaller of Bermuda's two lighthouses (Gibb's Hill, Bermuda's other light-house, is pictured on page fifteen), and has warned ships of danger since 1879. A replica of St. David's lighthouse blew up in the movie *The Deep!*, but the real thing remains to stand watch over the tricky Bermuda waterways.

(bottom) **Sainte Madeleine Lighthouse**, Quebec, Canada, guides ships through the mouth of the Saint Lawrence River near the village of Riviere Madeleine on the Gaspé Peninsula.

(overleaf) **Westport Lighthouse**, Gray's Harbor, Washington, was built in 1898. The spiral stairs shown here lead to the lantern room, the top of which is over one hundred feet from the ground, and 123 feet above sea level. The height of this lighthouse allows its beacon to be seen as far as twenty-three miles out to sea.

(top) **El Faro Viejo** (The Old Lighthouse) sits amid the lonely sand dunes of the Bermejo Sea and the Pacific Ocean, two miles west of Cabo San Lucas at the tip of the Baja Peninsula, Mexico.

(bottom) **Linterna Lighthouse**, an abandoned eighteenth-century lighthouse in the southeast of Spain on the Costa del Sol, near Cartagena.

(right) **Elbow Reef (Hope Town) Lighthouse** has warned sailors away from the extensive Elbow Reef off the coast of Abaco Island in the Bahamas since 1864. The construction of the lighthouse met with considerable resistance from local residents, even though the records for 1860 show an astounding average of about one wreck per month at Abaco alone. Before the lighthouse was built, about half the able-bodied men of Abaco Island made their living from "wracking" (salvaging) the wreckage of ships which went down in the shallow waters of Elbow Reef. Wracking was big business, as the recovered cargo was considered by the government to be "imported goods" and was sent to Nassau for auction. Between 1820 and 1880 there were as many as three hundred vessels officially licensed to search the reefs for ships to salvage. Wracking represented almost half of the colony's revenue, as the government took 15 percent of the profit gleaned from these wracking auctions. When England decided to build a lighthouse at Hope Town, local hostility overflowed, and the records show that some residents sank a supply barge and withheld fresh water from workers constructing the lighthouse. However, the workers finished their job, and today the lighthouse serves its function to guide ships away from Elbow Reef. It is still manned with a keeper and was fully renovated in the late nineties.

(left) Abandoned lighthouse on Cape Promontory, Wales.

(above) **Farol Moela Guaruga** in the state of São Paulo, Brazil.

At the foot of a lighthouse one finds darkness.

Spanish proverb

(top, left) **Rubjerg Fyr,** in rugged Rubjerg Knude, on the west coast of Jutland, Denmark, battles sand and wind. The lighthouse was taken out of operation in 1968 because the sand dunes grew taller than the seventy-five-foot-tall lighthouse itself, which of course ruined its use as a navigational tool. The lighthouse fittingly was converted to a museum dedicated to discussing the problem of sand migration, but had to close because the sand encroached ever closer. Attempts to keep the lighthouse free from sand were abandoned in 1994.

(top, right) Lighthouse on Belle-Île-en-Mer, France.

(right) **Farol Cabo Espichel,** found on Cape Espichel on the southwest coast of Portugal.

I lift my lamp beside the golden door.

From "The New Colossus"
by Emma Lazarus (1849–1887)
American poet

(left) **The Statue of Liberty** has lit New York Harbor since 1886, and though it serves more as a monument than a light station, it has greeted Americans, immigrants, and visitors to New York City as a beacon of pride for more than a century.

(top) Detail of the lamp at **Farol Castelhanos**, in the state of Rio de Janiero, Brazil.

(overleaf) **Point Loma Lighthouse** began operation in March of 1891, replacing the Old Point Loma Lighthouse, which was built too high on the bluff and was therefore often obscured by clouds. This "new" lighthouse is located at a lower point on the bluff. It is still in use and is therefore not open to tourists, but it can be seen from an overlook just a few yards south of the Old Point Loma Lighthouse (pictured on pages 6–7), which has been restored and is now part of Cabrillo National Monument.

(left) **Peggy's Cove Lighthouse**, perhaps the most famous lighthouse in Canada, has watched the waters of St. Margaret's Bay in Nova Scotia, Canada, since 1868. The lighthouse doubles as a post office, and letters sent from there receive a special lighthouse postmark. The history surrounding the name of the lighthouse remains a mystery. There are several versions of who Peggy's namesake might be—one simple explanation stems from St. Margaret's Bay. Since Peggy is a nickname often given to women with the name of Margaret, this is a natural extrapolation. Some say that Peggy was the wife of William Rodgers, an Irish immigrant, and that the cove was given her name in 1770 as a tribute to her. An intriguing story is that Peggy was the sole survivor of a horrible shipwreck, but another legend tells of a woman named Peggy who died in a shipwreck and whose body washed up on the shore nearby. Peggy's Cove is interesting not just for its name, but also for its archeology. The lighthouse is surrounded by immense granite ledges and boulders which are more than 400 million years old. A large monument to the men and women who've made their lives off the sea can be found in one of the rocks near the lighthouse. It depicts thirty-two fishermen, their wives and children, and the artist's vision of the legendary and mysterious Peggy.

(this page) **Farol Maceió**, in Maceió, Brazil, was built in 1856. The stairs shown here lead to the lantern room, which generates a powerful beacon that can be seen as far as forty-three miles out to sea.

(this page) **Split Rock Lighthouse**, on Lake Superior in Minnesota, is unusual, because although it is no longer in use, it remains a complete twentieth-century light station, with a tower, keeper's house, fog signal building, and oil house, all of which were erected in 1910. The United States Coast Guard built the light station in the days when iron ore shipments were ever present on Lake Superior. A single storm on November 28, 1905, endangered twenty-nine ships, many of which were the uninsured property of the steel company fleet, and two of which went aground on the rocks near where the lighthouse was eventually built. The lighthouse was deactivated in 1969, but it is now the focal point of Split Rock Lighthouse State Park. The light shines once again every year on November 10 to commemorate the loss of the *Edmund Fitzgerald* in a program which includes the reading of the names of all those who lost their lives in the terrible 1975 shipwreck.

(right) **Farol Cabo Frio** is located on the small island of Cabo Frio, about three hours by boat from the city of Rio de Janeiro in Brazil.

(overleaf) **Inishowen Head Lighthouse** at the northern tip of County Donegal, Ireland, has lit the mouth of the Lough Foyle since 1837.

(left) **Point Venus Lighthouse** is located on a picturesque black sand beach on Tahiti's northernmost point. Point Venus is the site where Captain James Cook observed the transit of the planet Venus across the sun in 1769, thus providing the point with a name. The area is rich with history, as Captains Wallis, Cook, and Bligh all explored the area after anchoring their ships behind the reef in Matavai Bay. Though a sign above the door reads "1867," the lighthouse was completed in 1868, and was built in part by novelist Robert Louis Stevenson's father.

(top) **Farol Aracaju**, in Aracaju, the capital of the state of Sergipe in Brazil. The lighthouse was built in 1888, and its beam reaches thirty-nine miles out to the Atlantic Ocean.

(bottom) **Maelvakkey Lighthouse** in Iceland.

(top) **Ogden Point Signal Lighthouse,** on Vancouver Island, British Columbia, Canada.

(bottom) **Farol São Marcos** in the city of São Luis, Maranhão, Brazil.

(right) The light on top of Stykkis Rock, Stykkisheimur, Iceland.

(overleaf) **Baily Light,** on Howth Head in County Dublin, Ireland, has existed in one form or another since 1667. Its first incarnation was as a small cottage-type coal burning lighthouse, which was replaced by a tower in 1790. In 1814, because the light was often obscured by fog and low cloud cover, the light was repositioned lower down on the peninsula, at Little Baily, and it remains there today. The tower was painted white until 1910, when it was stripped to its natural granite. The light flashes every fifteen seconds across Dublin Bay, and in 1997 it became the last of the Irish lighthouses to be automated.

And o'er them the lighthouse
    looked lovely as hope,
That star of life's
    tremulous ocean.

From "The Beacon"
Paul Moon James (1780–1854)
English author

(left) **Farol Calcanhar**, which shines on the waters near Touros in Brazil's northeastern state of Rio Grande do Norte, is the first South American signal sailors see as they cross the Atlantic Ocean from Europe.

(above) **South Pierhead Light**, South Haven, Michigan, was originally a wooden tower built in 1872, but the current cast-iron structure was constructed in 1903. The spire overlooks Lake Michigan at the mouth of the Black River and is accessed by a steel catwalk. The light remains active, casting its beacon for the many pleasure boaters who play in the waters of Lake Michigan.

(top) **White River Lighthouse**, near Whitehall, Michigan, on Lake Michigan at the mouth of the White River, was established in 1876 with the help of Captain William Robinson, an English sailor who settled in Michigan in the 1800s. Just after the Civil War ended, the Muskegon/White Lake area of Michigan was known as "The Lumber Queen of the World," and many ships sailed across the Great Lakes transporting lumber out of the area. Captain Robinson realized that the ships needed guidance, so even before an official light station was established at the mouth of the White River, he built fires on the beach to help ships find the channel. With Captain Robinson's assistance, a lighthouse was constructed in 1875, and he was named the first keeper of the newly established light station. Captain Robinson and his wife lived in the keeper's quarters for forty-seven years, raising eleven children there, and both Captain Robinson and his wife died in the house. The lighthouse is no longer in use except as a museum, but the live-in curator swears that the friendly spirits of Captain Robinson and his wife still live in the house. She hears Captain Robinson's footsteps and the thump of his cane as he makes the rounds late at night, and has found signs of Sara Robinson's help in her daily chores.

(right) **Charlotte-Genesee Lighthouse**, near Rochester, New York, sits where the Genesee River meets Lake Ontario. The octagonal light tower and its keeper's quarters make up the second oldest lighthouse on the Great Lakes, and both are listed on the National Register of Historic Places. The tower was built close to the lake in 1822, but over time it "moved" farther and farther away from the lake. In 1829, piers were built to prevent the formation of sandbars at the mouth of the river, so sand was instead deposited along the piers and a beach began to grow, leaving the tower farther from the lake each year.

(left) **Lobster Cove Head lighthouse** at Gros Morne National Park, Newfoundland, Canada, has lit the approach to the town of Rocky Harbour and the entrance of Bonne Bay since 1897. Before the lighthouse was built, residents who feared for fishing schooners which remained on the water after dark donated a pint of oil a week to a local fisherman who kept a light burning in his home. At the turn of the century, this cast-iron structure was constructed to ease the minds of family members by safely guiding the fishing boats to the refuge of the shore. Lobster Cove Head Lighthouse continues to shine its light for night travelers, but the keeper's house now features a public exhibit which interprets how people have harvested the local waters for more than four thousand years.

(above) **South Stack Lighthouse** is situated on a tiny islet known as South Stack Rock, separated from Holy Island, Wales by about one hundred feet of turbulent water. The ruggedly beautiful coastline is made of large granite cliffs rising sheer from the Irish Sea to almost two hundred feet above sea level.

(above) **Eldred Rock Light Station** sits on its own island (Sullivan Island) in Lynn Canal, near Haines, Alaska. It was established in 1906, and is the oldest surviving lighthouse in Alaska. Eldred Rock Light was automated in 1973, and is listed on the National Register of Historic Places.

(right) **Point Sur Lighthouse** has lit the precarious waters near Big Sur, California, since 1889. The wreck of the *Ventura* in 1875 helped to fuel mariners' pleas for a lightstation in the area—according to reports, a drunken captain allowed a ship to hit a cluster of rocks near Point Sur. Ironically, plans to build the lighthouse weren't welcome news to many of the people who lived along the coast, because although a shipwreck meant disaster to shipping companies and crew, it meant a new influx of supplies for the coastal residents. The powerful current ripped the ships apart, sending its foodstuffs, trade goods, and lumber to shore for beachcombers to pilfer.

(overleaf) **Tranoy Fyr** guides ships into the Vest Fjord in the chilly Norwegian Sea, keeping them safe from the many small, rocky islands which clutter the waters off the coast of Norway.

INDEX

Page numbers in **boldface** refer to photographs.

CREDITS

© **Pete Amass**: pp. 50 (left), 71

© **Tony Arruza**: pp. 21 (left), 24, 43 (top)

© **John Eagle**: pp. 66-67

© **Don Eastman**: pp. 8 (bottom), 15, 65, 74 (top)

© **Kathleen Norris Cook**: Back cover, pp. 6, 8 (top), 9, 22–23, 32, 33, 34–35, 40 (top), 41, 46 (top), 54–55

© **Ricardo Siqueira**: pp. 2–3, 14 (bottom), 18, 19, 29 (top), 36 (top and bottom), 38, 39 (top), 49, 53, 57, 59, 63 (top), 64 (bottom), 68

© **Britstock**:
    Cheryl Hogue; pp. 25, 37, 69
    Ronald Gorbutt; p. 70

© **Corbis**:
    Robert Holmes; p. 1
    Richard Cummins; pp. 7, 44–45, 60–61, 73
    Roger Garwood and Trish Ainslie; p. 10–11
    Steve Raymer; p. 12
    Gail Mooney; p. 13 (top)
    Danny Lehman; p.13 (bottom)
    Niall MacLeod; p. 14 (top)
    Yann Arthus-Bertrand; pp. 16–17, 26, 27 (top), 28
    Kevin Schafer; p. 21 (right)
    Wolfgang Kaehler; pp. 27 (bottom), 30–31
    Ron Watts; p. 39 (bottom)
    Kevin Fleming; p. 40 (bottom)
    Paul A. Souders; pp. 42, 64 (top)
    Michelle Chaplow; p. 46 (bottom)
    Bill Lisenby; p. 47
    Chinch Gryniewicz; Ecoscene; p. 48
    Patrick Ward; p. 50 (right)
    Tony Arruza; p. 51
    Dallas and John Heaton, Westlight; p. 52
    Layne Kennedy; p. 58 (bottom)
    Douglas Peebles; p. 62
    Hubert Stadler; p. 63 (bottom)
    Chris Rainier; p. 75

© **International Stock**:
    Edmund Nagele; cover
    Greg Johnston; pp. 20, 56
    Chad Ehlers; p. 29 (bottom), 76
    Andre Jenny; pp. 43 (bottom), 72
    Bob Firth; p. 58 (top)